Goal Setting Success:

The Blueprint To Setting Goals & Achieving Them

© **Copyright 2020 by Oscar Monfort - All rights reserved.**

This document is geared towards providing exact and reliable information in regard to the topic and issue covered. The publication is sold with the idea that the publisher is not required to render accounting, officially permitted, or otherwise, qualified services. If advice is necessary, legal or professional, a practiced individual in the profession should be ordered.

- From a Declaration of Principles which was accepted and approved equally by a Committee of the American Bar Association and a Committee of Publishers and Associations.

In no way is it legal to reproduce, duplicate, or transmit any part of this document in either electronic means or in printed format. Recording of this publication is strictly prohibited and any storage of this document is not allowed unless with written permission from the publisher. All rights reserved.

The information provided herein is stated to be truthful and consistent, in that any liability, in terms of inattention or otherwise, by any usage or abuse of any policies, processes, or directions contained within is the solitary and utter responsibility of the recipient reader. Under no circumstances will any legal responsibility or blame be held against the publisher for any reparation, damages, or monetary loss due to the information herein, either directly or indirectly.

Respective authors own all copyrights not held by the publisher.

The information herein is offered for informational purposes solely and is universal as so. The presentation of the information is without contract or any type of guarantee assurance.

The trademarks that are used are without any consent, and the publication of the trademark is without permission or backing by the trademark owner. All trademarks and brands within this book are for clarifying purposes only and are the owned by the owners themselves, not affiliated with this document.

Rituals Of The Rich & Famous

Free Success Tips, Strategies and Habits of The Rich & Famous

Four new strategies every week on how to be more productive, confident, and happy.

Join Successful Subscribers!

Do you have a clear vision for your life? Do you have a 5 year plan? Or does it feel like you're just drifting through life?

The truth is that most of us are just wishing that something good will happen to us.

Forget all the over-hyped, positive thinking and visualization stuff....

The key to getting what you want from life is to set clear, realistic and measurable goals. Goal setting is a scientifically proven way to restructure your brain cells and direct you towards the future you want.

However goal setting alone is not enough. Nice idea yeah, but many give up or work so hard without getting anywhere. The reality is that there is a science to the goal achievement process and it's not what you would think.

Instead of some half baked New Year's Resolutions the blueprint inside this book focuses on the process of actually achieving goals. From how to set goals in the first place to avoiding common roadblocks and easily navigating your journey to success.

In This Book You Will Discover;

- The Key To Setting Goals & Achieving Them
- The Goal Setting Method Used by Lady Gaga Which Took Her From An Unknown Gogo Dancer To An International Super-star
- Scientifically Proven Ways To Align Your Environment With Your Goals

- Easily Develop Habits That Lead to Huge Results
- Warren Buffett's 5 Step Success Rule
- Why Failure is Necessary & How to Embrace It
- How Taylor Swift Achieved Global Success Through Mentors (Without ever meeting them)
- The Simple Goal System Used by Google, Walmart, Spotify, Twitter & More
- How A Beekeeper Became The First Person To Climb Mount Everest
- Applying Behavioural Psychology To Set Goals You'll Actually Stick To

And Much, Much More….

Let's be honest, if you want success, you need to set goals and take action. Are you willing to do whatever it takes? If you're ready to turn your dreams into reality then start reading this book.

Table of Content

INTRODUCTION 1
WHAT IS GOAL SETTING? 4
HOW TO SET GOALS 9
EXAMPLES OF GOAL SETTING 24
BE RUTHLESS 27
TURN YOUR DREAMS INTO REALITY 31
MOTIVATION & TIME 36
NEVER GIVE UP 45
TEAMS & ACADEMIA & MORE 51
THE FEEDBACK LOOP 56
CONCLUSION 61
BONUS GOAL SETTING GUIDES 70

INTRODUCTION

Stefani Germanotta was born in New York, on March 28, 1986. From the age of four she began playing the piano. By fourteen years old she had written her first piano music and performed in a New York nightclub. A few years later she was just one of twenty students in the world to be granted early admission to the prestigious New York University's Tisch School of the Arts. Whilst there, she continued to elevate her songwriting skills and music. Funding her studies was not easy and to make ends meet, she took on various jobs. One of which included working as a gogo dancer where she learned about burlesque.

Fast forward to 2005 and she was briefly signed by the legendary Def Jam Records. However just a few months later she was dropped by the label. Being dropped motivated her to perform and refine her burlesque performances in venues around New York City. There she also collaborated with rock bands, and began her experimentation with other musical styles. In 2007 she began working as a songwriter at Interscope Records for other artists on the label, including Britney Spears and The Pussycat Dolls. After seeing her perform a burlesque show the R&B singer Akon signed her to his label to start recording her debut album, The Fame. The album received positive reviews and was a massive international success.

Lady Gaga knew she was a star way before the rest of the world did. She would repeat this to herself everyday saying. "'Music is my life and I'm going to make a number-one record,'" One day it became true, many times over. Until now she has had more than four number one albums plus countless top ten hits. Goal setting played a huge part in her success.

Goal setting is powerful.

It is about taking steps towards a future that you want. Do you ever feel like life just happens to you and it's out of your control? Maybe when something good happens you attribute it to good luck. Maybe you have a rough idea of what you want but you're not really sure how to get it. Well the answer to your curiosity can be found in goal setting. So often we don't live upto our full potential because we procrastinate.

Naturally we assume that we can do it at some point and that doesn't have to be now. But before you know it time passes you by. The years fly by. A year feels like a day. But a day should feel like a year. Life should be full. To become a success you will need to have some goals set. But the problem is that too many people are drifting through life. When you don't set goals then you're never going to live up to your full potential. Maybe you're working really hard but not getting anywhere worthwhile. This is because you're not spending time to think about what it is that you really want from life. Without setting specific objectives you end up going nowhere. Think about it like this, would you try to drive somewhere without a map or GPS? Goals are the destination and setting them is the map. A life without goals has no direction and is aimless. When you know your life purpose and turn your dreams into achievable goals and then act on them, you're guaranteed success.

My name is Oscar Montfort and I used to drift through life. With no clear goals I took what life gave me. Which was not always what I expected. Jaded and frustrated I found answers in goal setting. I successfully quit my job last year and have since seen my income grow and my hours shrink. Not only that but my health is excellent, I have great relationships and spend my time doing what I love. Goal setting gave me this blessed life. It gave me something to aim for. When you have a clear destination it heightens your awareness of how to get there. No doubt, challenges will come along the way but your mind will stay focused on your goal. That journey starts with the question. What do you really want in life? The answers to that question will present you with a path.

With a clear vision for your life it will focus your efforts to achieve what you want. Your mind is clear of the things that stress you out and focused on what matters. Goal setting allows you to set boundaries and push the distractions away. Setting goals that matter to you manifests those things into your life. In effect your life will be changed for the better. The difference between a successful person and one who is not is that most people are unsuccessful because they didn't define their goals in the first place. To be a winner, you need to define your goals and go to work on them.

Time is the great equalizer of rich and poor. It is your most valuable asset. When it is gone it can never be recovered. When you have goals your time can be managed much more effectively so that you don't have to waste precious time on things that may never benefit you. Goal setting allows you to allocate enough time for the things of most importance. Ultimately you are shaping your future. Goals help you to shape the destiny you wish for. The moment you set them, they become a plan for the future. No more wandering aimlessly in life, take control of your future. This gives us hope for the future. When you have hope it gives you motivation to work towards achieving it.

The truth is that achieving your goals is a journey. A journey that should be worthy and enjoyable. You need to enjoy it. There will be times where your motivation slides up and down over time. Goal setting is not just saying you want something to happen and wishing for it. You need to clearly define what you want and why. This book will show you how. We are all capable of achieving goals beyond our personal expectations. Believe me I'm proof of that. With goal setting you can raise the bar of your potential and push yourself to achieve things that before you only hoped was possible. Now if you don't already set goals then let this book show you how to begin. As you make goal setting a part of your life, you'll find your life accelerating.

Let's begin.

WHAT IS GOAL SETTING?

Goal setting is essentially about choosing a specific objective that you want to achieve within a specified time. Simply put, goal setting is the act of selecting a target that you want to achieve and through this we can measure ourselves. Success in life, work, relationships, health and everything else in between requires goal setting. When we have goals it gives our life purpose and something to strive for.

Understand that goals can be applied to any area of your life. They can include personal, health, business, romantic, spiritual, career and more. Those can be long or short term. The choice is yours and I'll show you how to make your goals happen. Setting the right goals with the right plans is going to give you the success that you want from life. Goals will give you focus, direction and motivation to wake up everyday and go after your life. They will keep you away from the stupid stuff and ultimately will determine if you're going to be successful.

Now setting a goal is easy because after all who doesn't want to make loads of money? Or have an amazing body? Or a relationship with the person of their dreams? The real challenge isn't setting the goal, it's about asking yourself are you willing to accept the sacrifices required to achieve that goal? Because going for a goal is going to require some sacrifices to achieve it. It's not all going to be glamorous and fun. For example olympic athletes who set goals to win a gold medal. Sure that's an amazing goal to go for. But behind achieving those few seconds of glory are years and years of struggle, discipline, dedication and hard work. Are you willing to do what it takes to achieve your goals?

Now it doesn't matter what age you are or what your circumstances are. Goal setting is about changing those circumstances and making your life better. Goals not only affect behaviour but they also affect your performance. It's proven that they give you more energy which will lead to a higher effort and this will increase the results in your life. When we are sufficiently challenged it helps to motivate and encourage us to perform at a higher level which in turn leads to a higher level of success. A well set goal will require you to make significant efforts. This is really important and beneficial because it will stretch your capabilities and grow you as a person. On your journey towards your goals you're going to meet many obstacles. Overcoming those obstacles will require persistence. Some goals may also require you to change and develop certain behaviours.

Goal setting focuses you on the actions and behaviours that you need to implement to achieve your goals. For example if you have a goal to save a certain amount of money it's going to influence you to be more smart with your money. To make better financial decisions. That's a step in the right direction and will give you the kind of life you want and cut out the stuff that you don't want. Just think of the colour red and you will see the colour red around you. Or for example if you set the goal to meet an attractive new partner then that's going to be more in your awareness. It will influence more of the right activities and actions towards achieving that. Once you start taking the right activities and actions you will build momentum. Just like a snowball gets bigger when it rolls down the mountain this will be the similar effect of you going towards your goals you become better and more effective.

Finally goals will build your character to become a more actualized person. Self mastery is a critical component of setting goals. It's about becoming the best version of yourself. Goal setting will help you to do that and much more.

Goal setting requires some essential skills in order to be successful. These are skills that can be learnt and developed through practice. Those will be discussed in more detail later on but for now let's take a brief look.

- *Planning*

Planning and organizational skills are crucial components of the goal achievement process.

- *Clarity*

Having clarity around your goals will definitely put you on the right pathway. If your goals are vague then it will be difficult to get motivated. You need a clear vision. Goals can be made more specific through:

- Quantification - making it measurable. For example "$10,000 per month" instead of "make more money"
- Enumeration - defining tasks that need to be completed in order to achieve a goal. For example, "run every morning, to lose 5kg"

- *SMART +*

Make your goals fit into the SMART framework. That is they should be specific (S), measurable (M), achievable (A), realistic (R), timebound (T) and positive (+).

- *Motivation*

Motivation is what will encourage us to achieve a goal. Without the motivation goals are destined to fail. Which means you need to have goals that positively motivate you. It is imperative that goals are important and relevant on a personal level.

- *Time Management*

Goal setting relies heavily on being able to manage time well.

- *Flexibility*

Not all your plans will go as you expect. Sometimes you might have to divert from the planned method and go in another direction. A flexible attitude is necessary in this regard.

- *Persistence and focus*

Just as much as your plans might not go as you expect. Obstacles will also come your way and your motivation will go up and down. At those times you're going to need to stay persistent, focused and keep moving forward. Onwards and upwards.

- *Challenging*

Effective goal setting means you should set goals that are a little bit out of your reach yet they are still attainable. This will challenge you and require you to improve yourself. In turn that will give you the motivation to push your skills forward to their limits.

- *Self-regulation*

Goal setting can be challenging. Goals will and should test you to do what you didn't think was possible before. That will cause you to grow and become better. During that process you need to be able to regulate and manage your emotions so that you can deal with the challenges. This requires self-regulation.

- Vision

Your goals should paint a clear picture in your mind's eye. That vision must inspire you and be crystal clear.

- *Feedback*

Finally you need to have a good feedback system in place. That can be both internal and externa. Track and measure your results. This can be by yourself or you can also have a mentor to help you. Ultimately you need to know how you're progressing.

HOW TO SET GOALS

What should your goals be? Good question. Well some people might think life is all about money. Or life is about having a good time. In reality life has so many components to it. This is why I recommend you set goals in specific areas of your life. You want to live a full life right? Sometimes your health might not be good but you finanacial your situation is good. Or maybe have great relationships now but your career is not where you want it to be. Having a more balanced view of your life will help you to celebrate the wins in different areas. Let's take a closer look at the areas of your life.

Goal Setting Step 1

There are many sections here for you to set some goals for yourself in. If you want to add more go ahead. Live a full life. Brainstorm here and if you get stuck use some of the question prompts. Set a timer for five minutes on each section. No censorship, write as fast as you can.

Health

Health is the most important section. Without good health nothing else is really possible. Brainstorm this area and to help you consider the following questions.

- How do you want to look? How do you want to feel? Maybe you want to leap out of bed everyday. Or look and feel years younger than you really are. Whatever it is, write it down.

- How much do you want to weigh?

Maybe you want to lose a few kilos. Or maybe you want to bulk up and pack on the muscles.

- What do you want to accomplish?

That could be accomplishments such as lifting a certain amount of weight, competing in an event, running a distance or getting a martial arts grade.

- Are there any cosmetic procedures or surgeries you want?

Perhaps you want to enhance the way you look or take care of something that really bothers you. Don't be afraid to acknowledge this. If it's what you really want and not something just to fit in then write it down. It could be something simple as getting your teeth whitened or having a weekly facial.

- How often would you like to exercise?

Maybe you hate to exercise and want to do the least amount for the most gain. Or maybe you're a gym rat and you want to go all in.

- Are there any sports you want to try? Do you want to join a team or start up a new sport?

Relationships

Relationships give meaning to our life. Having someone to share life moments with makes life much more enjoyable. Think about what you're looking for in your relationships. Take five minutes to brainstorm and use the following questions to help you find clarity.

- What kind of relationship are you looking for?

Maybe you just want to date for a while. Or maybe you want to improve your existing relationship by committing to more dates, romance and better communication. Whatever you want.

- Do you want a better sex life?

Maybe this has been a concern of yours for a while and you want to improve it.

- Do you want a better romantic life?

Maybe your relationship has gone stale and it needs some new life breathed into it. Think about how you want to improve it.

- Do you want to get married? Have children?

Friends

Just like relationships, friends are equally important to living and sharing our best moments in life. Think about what you want here. Consider the following questions.

- What kind of social life do you want?

Maybe you want to attend more meetups, seminars and be out there everyday.

- What kind of friends do you want in your life?

Maybe you're tired of your old friends and you want to meet new people who inspire you. It could be meeting up with more like minded people on a regular basis or finding a mentor.

- What kind of social habits or skills would you like to develop?

Maybe it's simply saying hi to more people or working on your confidence.

Family

Family is another important part of our life. We need to give it the right amount of attention and not neglect. Family is important, it needs priority. Think about how you want your family life to be.
- Do you want to spend more time with your family? How much time and how often?

That could be moving closer to them or setting aside time each month or year to spend with them.

- Are there activities you want to do with your family? When? How often?

Maybe you love taking beach holidays with your parents or you just want to meet with your family for a weekly dinner.

- Do you want to have your own family?

Be specific about what you want. If you want ten kids then write it down. Dare to dream big.

Finance

Finance and money are the easiest things to quantify. They can help us directly measure our success and are a great indicator of it. Take the time to be specific about what you want. Dare to have big goals. Brainstorm and consider the following bullet points.

- How much money do you want to earn per month, per year? What would you like your salary to be?

Maybe you want to double your income and work less hours. Or maybe you want to get a better deal or even to quit your job. Would you like your paycheck to increase by a certain amount?

- How much money do you want to have saved?

Saving and growing your money is really important. Rainy days come and ultimately wealth is measured by net worth. Set what you want to go for.

- What investments would you like to make?

Having a bunch of money saved is good. But why not have it work for you? Study and research the most profitable and safest ways to invest. Make sure you understand any investment you make before you commit to it.

- Would you like to be completely debt-free?

If there are debts that bother you then write them out.

- Would you like to adopt positive beliefs about money?

Maybe you have some limiting beliefs around money that need fixing. Identify them.

- How many streams of income would you like to create? Would you like to start a business?

Maybe you're tired of the rate race and would like to build your own business on the side. Or you might have a great idea and want to go all in on it.

- When would you like to retire (at what age)?

- Would you like to be a multimillionaire?

Career

Most of our lives are spent working. But most of us are not working in jobs we enjoy. Think about your career and what you want to be, do and achieve. Take the time to brainstorm and consider the following questions.

- What do you want to achieve in your career?

Maybe right now you're not happy. You want to quit your job and change to a new career. Or it could be something like getting a promotion or making moves to start a business.

- Are there any professions out there that interest you?

We only live once so spend it doing what you enjoy. Don't chase the money, chase the passion and the money will follow.

- Do you want to go back to study or learn a useful work skill?

You're never too old or experienced to learn new things. That could mean completely reinventing yourself and going back to study a new skill. Allow yourself to make that possible.

Travel, passions and adventure

Travel, passions and adventures are the things that make us feel alive. They are what we love to do. Set your imagination free.

- Where do you want to travel to? How long do you want to spend there?

Travel is a great way to spend time. Think about where you most want to go. Maybe you want to spend a year backpacking or just a few weeks on a caribbean beach.

- What adventures do you want to go on?

Maybe you always wanted to jump out of a plane. Or climb a mountain. Dare to dream.

- How do you want to spend your free time?

Maybe you have always loved sailing and you want to spend your weekend out on the seas. Or maybe you love golf and want to be out on the course.

- What hobbies do you want to try?

Think about the hobbies you've always been curious about. Maybe you want to make music or learn to sing. Or maybe you want to learn how to cook.

Lifestyle

Lifestyle is about the quality of life you live. From the clothes you wear to the cars you drive, to the house you live in. Think big and set some goals.

What kind of place do you want to live in?
Maybe you want to live in a cottage in the countryside. Or maybe you want a fancy downtown apartment.

How would you like to travel?
Maybe you hate driving cars and you want a speed bike. Or maybe you want a new Porsche or you just want to be chauffeured around. Or even travel business class.

What kind of clothes do you want to wear?
Maybe being dressed in the latest designer fashion is important to you. Or maybe it's something as simple as looking good in nice fitting clothes.

Learning

Throughout life it's important to never stop learning

- Do you want to learn a new language?

Ever wanted to travel somewhere and speak with the locals. Considering learning a new language it can be an awesome skill to be able to communicate in a foreign country.

- Do you want to go back to study?

Maybe there is a hot new course you want to learn. Or you want to complete a masters.

- Do you want to learn anything else?

That could be anything from cooking to dressmaking to dancing. Whatever you want to learn, do it.

Spirituality/ Mental health

Mental health represents our state of mind. This is just as important as our physical body. Actions begin with thoughts and in order to be taking the right actions we need a healthy mind. Plus we need to be able to appreciate and enjoy life. Brainstorm and consider the following points. For some of us our faith is really important. For some of us we are curious about spirituality and faith. Or if it's not important to you then don't worry about it. But if you're curious or committed, take the time out to think about what you want. Brainstorm and consider the following.

- How do you want to feel?

Maybe you're tired of feeling depressed and you want to fix that. Or maybe you want to have a better attention span. Write down the things that bother you about mental health and set goals to fix them. Alternatively write out the ways you want to feel day to day.

- What activities do you want to do to improve your mental health?

Maybe you have always wanted to try meditation or brain training looks like a good idea to you. It could even be keeping a journal. Do a Google search to find some of the best ways to improve your mental health.

- Are you curious about any religions or spirituality?

Maybe you have always had a burning desire to seek out more knowledge on a spiritual journey. Whatever it is, take the path.

- Have you thought about doing a retreat or immersion?

Going on a retreat or immersion program can be one of the best ways to grow your faith and also improve your mental health. It could be something as simple as a yearly three day retreat.

Giving

Finally giving is really an important part of your goals. Some say the secret of living is giving. As you become more successful it's important to give something back and help others to achieve success. Brainstorm how you can give back?

- Are there any charities you want to support and how?

Maybe you want to set up a regular donation. Or even go and volunteer.

- What ways can you like to help others?

Again that could be donation, volunteering or even teaching valued skills to those in need.

Goal Setting Step 2

Ok so by now you should have a pretty big list of goals. Actually you should have a huge list of goals! Don't worry about the size of it too much though. Having a big list is better because ultimately we want to be living a full life. Now what I want you to do is to go through those lists of goals and next to them simply write, m, 3, 6, y, 5, 1. Those numbers and letters indicate the amount of years or months that you expect to achieve those goals. So for example;

- m = one month
- 3 = three months
- 6 = six months
- y = one year
- 5 = five years
- 10 = ten years or more.

Don't worry about being too exact just give a rough estimate. Take five to ten minutes to complete this activity. When you are done you should have a list with all the categories of time.

Organize

At this point I would suggest that you start to put your goals into some kind of Excel sheet. Personally my writing is ugly, so for me it works well to put my goals into Google sheets. However if you like to keep things more natural and you have some beautiful handwriting then by all means keep it inside of a notebook. Either way create a new page for each of the goal headings and then organize them by time.

Choose your top one year goals for each of the main categories. Look at all the one year goals in each category and select the ones that make you the most excited. Below those put like the short-term goals then at the very bottom the long-term goals. Those long-term goals will be a bit more vague but they will give you an overall picture of exactly what you're looking for long term.

Next, eliminate any goals that are not so important. Focus only on the goals that are most important to you. Put any others on the back burner in a tab somewhere. You can start to prioritise those with simple things such as A, B, or C.

Get SMART +

With your main one year goals in mind use the S.M.A.R.T. protocol which is a great system to help you move towards your goals and achieve them. It's essentially a framework that allows you to make sure your goals are optimised based on different properties.

Specific

Goals need to be specific otherwise it's just pie in the sky. That's not going to motivate you or drive you in the right direction. To help you make your goal specific try to answer the following questions.

- What is it that you want to accomplish?
- Why is your goal important?
- Who is involved?

- Where is the goal located?
- Which resources are required?

In addition going back to the earlier chapter consider quantification and enumeration.

- Quantification - making it measurable. For example "lose 5kg" instead of "look good"
- Enumeration - break the goal into specific steps. For example "invest in an index fund to grow my net worth"

Measurable

To keep you motivated, on track and making progress you need to have measurable goals. When you're able to assess and measure your progress it will help you to stay focused, meet your deadlines and get excited about moving closer to achieving your goal. In order to turn your goal into something measurable, consider the following questions

- How much?
- How many?
- How will I know when my goal is accomplished?

Example

Let's say your goal is to get a promotion at your company. That can be measured by taking on the necessary training and then finally getting that promotion.

Achievable

True goals need to be challenging but they should not be completely unrealistic. The perfect goals should stretch your abilities yet still be possible. For example if you're a middle-aged guy then breaking the 100m world record is rather unrealistic. But you could for example work towards breaking your own records or even local ones. To help you set an achievable goal consider the following questions.

- How realistic is this goal based on my current situation?
- Realistically, could I accomplish this goal?
- What sacrifices would I have to make?
- Am I willing to make those sacrifices?

Tip
You can achieve much more than you think so don't be afraid to go for it. When I first started making money online I was realistic and set the goal to make just $1 online. When I achieved that it motivated me to shoot a bit higher. I kept doubling and going higher until I reached something that at the beginning was way beyond my wildest dreams. Start small and keep growing.

Relevant

Make sure that your goals matter to you and align with your vision for your life. On the journey towards your goals you will likely need support from people and your environment. Make sure they are aligned with your goals and also who you are as a person. If they don't then you need to consider making changes to either your goals, the people around you or your environment. Are you willing to do that? To make sure that your goals are relevant consider the following questions.

- Does this motivate me?
- What will it require??
- What kind of people could help me?

- What kind of environment do I need to be in?
- Am I willing to do what it takes?
- Is now the right time?

Example
Maybe you have the dream to travel the world or to visit ten countries in the next six months. However if the whole world is on lockdown for whoever knows how long then that is going to be impossible. In that case you might want to either delay that goal or to change it to something more relevant. For example, planning and saving or travelling within your home country.

Time-bound

In the end everyone needs to have a target date for their goals. A deadline for you to focus on and work towards. This will light a fire underneath you and motivate you to prioritise what gets results. Work either expands or contracts according to how much time is set for it. Be realistic about this but also make it a challenge for yourself. To turn your goal into something time based and answer the following questions.

- When is a realistic but challenging time to achieve this goal?
- What can I do right now?
- What is possible 1 months from now?
- What is possible 6 months from now?

Example
Maybe you're looking to compete in a small local bodybuilding competition. You want to get on the stage and look your best. Today that could involve going to the gym and eating clean.

In one month that could mean bulking your physique up through a high protein intake and heavy lifting. In six months it could be cutting down, losing fat and getting a toned body. During the process you could be taking pictures and measuring your results every month, week and so on.

+ Finally make your goals positive and present

The human mind is particularly sensitive to negativity and positivity. It's been proven that it's best to put your goals into the positive, present tense. Instead of having goal statements such as "I don't want to be fat" you need to be more positive and state something such as "I look and feel my best" so take a look at your goals and turn anything that looks negative into something positive in the present. Having them in the present tense also makes them more believable and less vague. When you look at your goals they should inspire you and motivate you to go for them.

EXAMPLES OF GOAL SETTING

Ok so if you struggled with the last chapter then I want you to take a look at this chapter. Here I'm going to give you some examples of goal setting. But if you didn't struggle with the last chapter and you're already well on your way then you can ignore this chapter and skip to the next one. Anyway I suggest you take a look either way.

Health

Susan is not really happy with the way she looks and feels. After a shower she looks in the mirror and isn't happy with what she sees. A little bit too much fat around the sides and a little too many wrinkles. In her mind she wants to "look younger and fitter". That's great but it's not really specific, measurable or time based. Although it is achievable and relevant so at least two boxes are ticked. Now on the time side of things this could be a great one year goal. She could already start making it specific by taking a look at her current age and height. Then by just doing some Google searches for people or celebrities of similar ages and heights that she wants to look like. She can find out what their weight and routines are. Then she has a rough idea of the weight she wants to be and what actions are required. Ok so that's one and then she can start to enumerate on that and figure out the right steps. Plus she now has something to measure and a strong vision to guide her forwards.

Relationships

For the last two years of his relationship Brian has not been happy. He always argues with his wife Mary. Ever since the kids left home it's like they are always clashing and getting in each other's ways. Brian and Mary still love each other but it's not realized enough. Frustrated, Brian decides to take action and make it a priority to bring the love back to their relationship. Recognizing this is the first step and the motivation is there. Brian talks with Mary about the times they cherished before the kids were born. The walks together, visiting people and going out for dinners. They agree to now make it a priority to have more unique and special moments together. Brian successfully set a goal. He made it specific and measurable because he can count how many special moments he shares with his wife. Plus it's completely relevant and achievable. Together they can work on expanding those moments to better and more grand activities. This will bring the love back to the relationship.

Finance

William had drifted from job to job for the past six years. Sometimes he would make a decent amount of money but then there would be months of low wages and he would just end up spending the savings. He hated relying on being an employee. Fed up he looked for a new way. He did his research and was inspired by people making money online and being their own boss. He decided that he wanted to build his own source of income and to be completely location independent. His vision was to be financially and location independent within one year. The next step for him was to make it more specific. He set about making a realistic income and this could be measured to make sure he was on target. That figure was always achievable for him and when he hit that target he would increase it. This helped to keep him motivated. Plus it was time bound. In addition he made sure to always keep his goal set in the positive tense so that his mind was inspired.

Learning

Claire was finishing up her bachelor of arts at Cardiff University. For the summer she planned to volunteer at a local school in Thailand. Claire had never been to Thailand before and she decided it would be a good idea to learn the language. With an idea in mind, Claire set herself the goal to become fluent in conversational Thai language within three months. The goal fit well within the SMART protocol. It was specific and could be measured by how well she conversed. Achievable and realistic also yes because it wasn't so unrealistic that there was not enough time to learn. Finally it was time bound by three months. Next the plan and feedback system could easily fit into place as she could brainstorm the actions and feedback points for the goal. For example she could use apps, books and then measure her progress by how well she conversed with locals or graded on tests.

<u>BE RUTHLESS</u>

One of the biggest obstacles to achieving your goals is the other goals that you have. Each goal is competing for time and attention from each other. When you commit to one goal you're taking the focus and energy from another. To achieve your most important goals requires a ruthless attitude. Take advice from Warren Buffett who has been consistently ranked as one of the most wealthy people in the world. Clearly he knows how to manage and spend his time each day. To help his employees decide upon their main priorities he uses a three step productivity strategy.

The first step is to write down your goals. Since we've already done that we can skip ahead to step two - choose your top five goals. Go through the lists of the different goals you set and choose the five most important to you.

Step three, anything that you did not choose is not urgent. These goals should be avoided at all costs otherwise they will just take your time and focus away from your main goals. Wasting time on secondary goals is the main reason you have half-finished projects instead of completed ones. Eliminate ruthlessly and force yourself to focus on what matters.

The Four Burners Theory

Imagine a cooking stove with four burners on it. Each burner represents a quadrant of your life. This is a concept known as The Four Burners Theory. The Four Burners Theory states that for you to be successful you have to cut off one of your burners. But to be really successful you have to cut off two of your burners.

- Burner one represents your family
- Burner two represent your friends
- Burner three represents your health
- Burner four represents your work

Now I know what you're thinking. There must be some way that I can succeed and keep all of those four burners running, right? Maybe you could combine two. For example you could start a business with your wife and kids and then you can combine family and work. Or you could switch jobs to be a fitness instructor and then you're making money and taking care of yourself at the same time right? Sure that's all good but you're still not facing the issue at hand. Which is that life is full of trade offs. If you really want to excel in one area then you need to make sacrifices in another area. For example if you want to be a family man then you're going to need to step back from your career ambitions a little bit. Or if you want to do it the other way round then you are going to be spending less time at home and sacrifice moments with your family. You can divide time equally amongst those burners but you have to accept that you won't reach your full potential in all of those areas.

Which means you need to make choices. Do you want to live a life that is out of balance but very successful in one area? Or would you rather live a balanced life but never truly live up to your full potential in any of those areas? Now don't worry because there are some ways you can still excel and be balanced. One way is that you can outsource some of those burners. There are so many small things in our lives that we can outsource. We can get delivery food so that we don't have to cook. We can pay someone to take care of our laundry. We can hire a nanny to take care of our kids. We can pay a virtual assistant to take care of tasks that we don't want to do in our business. Things like this free us to spend time on more meaningful activities. Essentially it keeps the burning running without you wasting unnecessary time on it.

Another option you have concerns the time available in your life. When thinking of The Four Burners Theory it can be frustrating to think, "if only I had more time". Well the way around that is to maximise the time you have. Each of us have our own set of constraints and limitations on our time. Maybe that's working from nine to five every day. Or having family, exercise and various other commitments every day. What you need to ask yourself is, am I being as effective as possible here? For example if you only have one hour to work out each day ask yourself what is the most effective way to reach my goal during this time? Or if I have my evenings to spend with my family what is the best way to spend quality time with them?

Be ruthless with your self examination. Lines of questioning like this focus us to make the most of the time available. Instead of worrying about negativity and not having enough time your focus will be on the quality of time spent. After all isn't it better to spend one hour of quality romantic time with your partner then an evening of watching meaningless stuff on Netflix? Wouldn't it be better to smash a workout in thirty minutes as opposed to scrolling through your phone intermittently during an average one hour workout?

Finally another way to manage the four burners theory is by breaking time into the seasons of life. Break the balances between the burners to different periods of time where you focus more on one particular area during a period of time. That can change throughout your life. For example in your twenties and thirties you're probably going to be single and so it's going to be easier to hit the gym and chase your career ambitions. That's when those health and work burners will be full whilst family and friends are turned down. Then years later you might want to turn down those burners and turn up the family burners. Later on you might turn them up again as your children grow up and you have more time to spend on work pursuits. It could even mean periods of immersion. Such as taking out three months to write your new book. Or a year off to spend time with your family and newborn child. You can have those other burners in maintenance mode and always come back to them later on.

TURN YOUR DREAMS INTO REALITY

Goals can seem daunting but if you have an actionable plan in place it can increase the chances of making them much more likely to achieve. Plans are the blueprint to get you from where you are now to where you want to be in the future. A plan of action consists of all the actions, activities, habits and so on that are essential to successfully achieving your goal. This turns your goal into quantifiable actions that can be mapped out on a timeline. Included inside will be ordered necessary steps required to achieve your goals. You can break that huge overwhelming goal into single or multiple goals.

It's been proven that you're much more likely to stick to your goals when you have a specific plan for them. Think about the when, where and how. There are specific benefits to planning. Number one it improves your productivity. A plan is going to stop you wasting your time and energy on unnecessary tasks. Every minute you spend will be on executing something important. This will also give you more focus and help you to feel more in control of your life. In turn this affects your confidence because you're moving forward and it proves that your plans are working. Finally it gives you greater self-awareness because it helps you to understand yourself and your life priorities.

With your goals in mind you need to figure out the daily, weekly and monthly activities that you need to complete in order to make them happen. Select your goals and break them down into clearly defined steps. If you followed the steps before and you set SMART goals then it's going to be easy for you to break your goals down into actionable steps. Brainstorm and list every action step that needs to happen for you to achieve your goal. Figure out the people resources and materials that you need to complete your goal. Identify the daily or weekly habits that will move you closer towards your goal. For example if you want to get ripped then that's going to the gym and eating clean everyday. Or if you want to save more money than that's measuring your daily and weekly spending. Select what actions need to happen from the first to the last. Make sure that all of the actions are relevant and attainable in regard to your goal. If the action seems too big or overwhelming then it can be broken down into smaller actions.

- Work backwards, step by step from achieving your goal
- Brainstorm and list every action that needs to happen
- Figure out the people, resources and materials that you need
- Identify the daily, weekly or monthly habits that will move you closer
- Set time frames and use a calendar to help you

Along with having a deadline for your goal you also need a time frame for each action within your goal. This will ensure you are consistently progressing towards your goal. For each action step, assess what's required and then consider the amount of time that you need to complete the action. Be realistic and think about all of the obstacles and activities involved when you're selling a timeframe. Then set dates for each action and put those into your calendar to remind you.

Keep your plans together in some kind of planner. You should be looking at your goals everyday and reviewing them. Personally I recommend Google sheets and a calendar. This allows me to check in on my goals everyday either on my mobile or laptop from wherever I am in the world. I can update the goals as I progress. I recommend you keep a tab for each of your goals. So on one tab for example you could have health goals, then another finance and so on. On each of those tabs you can break down those goals into the actions you need to take each day, week, each month and so on. Monitor your progress on an available column.

Habits

Habits are automatic actions which means that not much thought goes into them. This makes it easy for you to quickly accomplish goals with ease. For example if you develop the habit of going to the gym everyday then that's a huge win for you. Or if your goal is to be more confident and you make it a habit of talking to strangers then that is an excellent habit.

Taking things further we can stack our habits. Stacking habits means that when we take one particular action it causes us to take another particular action. For example when you make your morning coffee it's a trigger for you to meditate. This then triggers you to do some stretching. Through habit stacking you can really start to implement a fully blown plan moving towards your goals with little effort!

Align Your Environment With Your Goals

To give yourself a good advantage, make your environment support your goals. Our decisions are often based on the environment that we find ourselves in. The decisions we make both personally and professionally are influenced by the options that are around us. For example if you use your mobile phone as an alarm clock then you'll be more likely to check your notifications when you wake up. If you hang out with people that like to get wasted every weekend then you're more likely to drink. If you have a huge 50inch TV inside your bedroom then you're more likely to spend most of your time watching it. Get the point?

Now those are all environments that can have negative implications on your life. So why not become more conscious of your environment and how it affects you? For example if health is important to you then make sure you live close to a gym or have some exercise equipment nearby. Make sure that you have healthy food options in your place. If you are tired of getting wasted every Friday night then set up something more productive to do such as a night class or going on a date with someone you like.

Try to boil things down to the simplest of essence and cut out the noise. If you have tons of distractions around you all the time it's going to make it very difficult to focus on what's important. Eliminate those decisions and distractions. Sometimes you might have to remove certain things completely. Maybe that's blocking certain websites on your browser. Or it's about limiting the kind of food that you're going to eat. Be ruthless.

Keep an organised and tidy environment. There have been numerous studies proving that untidy environments distract us from what we're doing. For this reason you should maintain a clean and tidy workspace. Make sure everything is in order and this will help you to stay focused. Every minute of your day matters so establish an optimised environment. Clear up your desk, put things away and organise your notes. In the same regard you need to eliminate mental distractions. Those can be the smallest thing such as background noise or having multiple tabs open on your computer. Or if you have people that are constantly interrupting, telephone calls, texts and so on then remove those distractions. Establish some boundaries and rules during your working hours. Maybe that means deleting social media and going somewhere that will allow you to be more productive.

MOTIVATION & TIME

Now excuse the hype and I don't want to be too unrealistic about it but I want to stay something. Most goals are possible to achieve if they are somewhat realistic. The reason why people are unsuccessful with goal setting is that they have a vague romantic idea of a goal. Maybe they read a motivational quote and got super motivated but never followed through. Again we come back to the SMART theory which is to say that you need to stick with the real, actionable specific goals.

Motivation is one of the biggest influences on successfully achieving a goal. Goals get people started and motivation gives them the energy to get things done. The combination results in success. The psychologist Edwin Locke in the 1960s proposed the theory of motivation in goal setting. His theory states that goal setting and task performance are linked to each other. Essentially this states that by having challenging goals your motivation will be higher.

You are your own best motivator and your motivation must come from within yourself. Regardless of encouragement, the only one who can achieve your goals is you. But how do you stay motivated? Here's how:

- *Set boundaries*

Be realistic here. True, you can work your face off but at some point you're going to get burned out. You need to be able to push yourself hard but you don't want to get so burned out that you never want to go again. For example if you're trying to lose weight maybe you run two days in a row and then the next day you have off or maybe you have a cheat day on a Sunday. Or maybe you're working so much on a project and then take time off to spend with your lover. Set yourself some simple boundaries and that will keep you motivated because you know that there will be a break coming up instead of endless work.

- *Break it down*

There's a famous saying "how do you eat an elephant? One bite at a time." Think about your goals in the same way. Big goals need to be taken one step at a time. Say for example if your goal is to be a business owner then you need to set some small actions first such as research, cutting down your hours, investing and so on. Think what your goal is and break it down into more manageable pieces. You should have done this in the chapter before but I just want to push that point home again because it will keep you motivated with small wins.

- *Minimize distractions*

Distractions will keep you from your goals. Nothing will get done that is meaningful. If you find yourself constantly distracted then maybe you're not very motivated by your goals and you need to revisit them. Otherwise you can minimize your distractions through elimination. The truth is focus is not really about optimization it's more about subtraction. So for example if you have things distracting you such as the TV or social media then you can block them or remove them from your environment. Again as we discussed, optimize your environment to have less distractions and you'll be able to get more done.

- *Education*

A thirst for knowledge is an excellent quality to have. Many times people get fed up and give up because they feel like they're not intelligent enough to achieve their goal. That is simply just a matter of education. If you feel you're not progressing fast enough just ask yourself do I have the appropriate knowledge? Incidentally you don't want to get lost in knowledge. Taking action is the most important step. But if there are areas that you feel that you don't have the adequate knowledge in then get educated. Study the relevant books, enroll yourself in a course or even hire a mentor and acquire all the relevant knowledge.

- *Waste no time*

Start right now on your goals. The best thing you can do for any goal that you set it to take a definitive action right away. If you want to get fit and healthy, go do some push ups right now. If you want to meet the partner of your dreams, sign up for an online dating site or go out and start meeting people. If you want to make money online then start researching how to do that. Do it now! Light the fire underneath you and take action right away. Waste no time and you will become motivated by your actions.

- *Embrace failure*

Failure is a part of success. Ask any successful person and they'll probably tell you that their failures by far outweigh their successes. The difference between them and the people who don't achieve their goals is that the latter give up. The successful realize that failure is part of the equation and it doesn't affect their motivation. It just makes them more motivated to try again and succeed at all costs. Think about it like the stock market. The only time you lose is when you sell (give up).

Time Management

Time management skills are crucial in goal setting. A person who manages their time wisely has a much better chance of achieving their goals than one who doesn't. If you don't have good time management skills then you might make some small progress towards your goals but you will never achieve your best results. Your best results rely on effective time management. Whether you're young or old time is the greatest equaliser for all of us. Yet so many people fail to achieve their goals because they didn't manage their time well. They procrastinated, they didn't prioritise and they didn't put together a proper time management plan. Essentially they wasted time, but life is too short for you to waste time.

Time management will give you more control over how you spend every moment of your life allowing you to spend more time doing what you love and what gets results. Doesn't that sound good? Of course it does, because ultimately that's how you can achieve your goals. There really are no negatives, only benefits. Benefits such as less procrastination. Having a schedule will provide you with a framework to go for what's really important to you and to cut out those things that are taking you away from your purpose. Stick to a good plan and your calendar. Then you can start to become really effective, implement a routine and build successful habits. When there's less procrastination in your life you're more likely to meet deadlines, get things done and achieve your goals.

Additionally this will cause you to work smarter. Through practice you'll be able to implement proper time management and set realistic deadlines which will give you the motivation to push forward when you achieve them. In turn you become more accountable for yourself and your results because you'll be analysing your own time spent. Through this time management and measurement you'll be able to tune into what gives you the best results and in turn have even better time management.

A side benefit of good time management skills is that you will be less stressed because you will have more free time to chill out and relax. Going at full speed all the time is going to eventually burn you out. You need time to unwind and let your brain cool down. Make sure you are living a well balanced life. Take breaks and avoid burnout. Good time management skills and techniques will allow you more time to focus on taking care of your mental health which is at the core of being a successful goal achiever. This lifts a burden of stress and anxiety from your shoulders. We need to be driven but also calm and collected to achieve our goals. To help you practice better time management here are some helpful tips.

- *Know your goals*

First and foremost make sure your goals are crystal clear. The earlier chapters should have helped you to ensure your goals meet those requirements. Now if you're still unsure then go back and do the exercise again. Otherwise you'll just be shooting for some vague concepts and that will cause a lot of procrastination. Make sure they meet the SMART criteria: Specific, Realistic, Achievable, Realistic, Time-Bound.

- *Track your time*

In order to be effective you need to understand where your time is being spent. Now you don't need to do this all the time. But I would suggest that for one week you track every hour of the day. You can set an alarm on your phone to go off every hour to remind you to write down what you are doing at that moment. Keep a log of it all. At the end of the week you can analyze where your time was spent, what you accomplished and if your time was well spent. Are you happy with the results? Do you need to improve? Are there activities that need to be removed? I suggest you do this every few months or so to make sure that you keep becoming more effective in the way you spend your time.

Prioritise

Every day you need to be working on your goals. By now you should have your goals mapped out in a planner. Every day you're going to need to set some tasks and actions to take towards achieving your goals. What I recommend you do is that at the end of every day or in the morning go through those goals and write down the top six most important things that you need to get done. Limit yourself to just six things. That will really trigger you to be hyper focused on what's a priority and what's really important to you.

Next pull up those six tasks and concentrate only on the first task. Do not stop working until that task is complete. Upon completion you can move on to the next task. Approach the whole list in the same fashion, never moving on to another task before you have completed the one task. At the end of the day you should have completed all of the six actions. If you haven't don't worry, put them onto the next day's plan and keep grinding towards success.

Earlier I mentioned choosing your six most important tasks to do for the next day. Well this is all about making priorities. Going further on that, the first action should be one of the hardest things to do and also the most beneficial. At the start of your day you will be at your freshest with full willpower.

Place your activities into four different sections based on urgency and importance. Just write out a box with four sections for each of those parts and then you can enter your actions. Alternatively you can use the simple prioritising method on a list. Write a number or letter next to each item and then organize by ascending priority. Use the time management quadrant below to help you prioritize.

Urgent and important (do)	Not urgent but important (plan)
Urgent but not important (delegate)	Not urgent and not important (eliminate)

- *Set time limits*

Some activities can go on forever if you let them. Things like checking emails or running advertising campaigns can just consume so much time. Instead it's better to limit the time spent. Block out time to do those activities and then set a timer. Work on those activities until that timer goes off. Not only will this give you hyperfocus but it will also create an excellent management of your time.

- *Say no*

Protecting your time is crucial. Sometimes it's ok for you to say no. For example if your boss asks you to do something that's not particularly urgent you might want to tell him that this is going to take you away from doing more meaningful activities. Instead delegate it. Or maybe your friends ask you out to drink beer but you want to work on your business. If there are projects not working out with people don't be afraid to walk away. By saying no to certain things it will free you up to focus your efforts on the things that matter.

Flexibility

As we discussed earlier when you set a goal you also create a plan to get there. But that plan shouldn't be so rigid that it doesn't have flexibility for unexpected opportunities and obstacles along the way. There's a famous quote that says the map is not the territory. This is a metaphor that can be applied to goals and planning The plan is the map but that doesn't mean it accurately reflects what's going to happen in real life. Things will happen that are unexpected. To deal with those we need to be flexible and sometimes take a different pathway. Or sometimes adjust your goal to maybe get something much better. Always be open to those opportunities and flexible on your path.

Stay fresh

Finally I want to tell you something that's pretty important. Stay fresh without judgment and without ego. It can be easy to get jaded and want to give up when things don't go the way you want. But if you can keep a clean slate in your mind that can really help to easily bring new opportunities to you.

Multi billionaire Richard Branson says "think like a child to get a head". Richard Branson is quite a unique person. After dropping out of school at the age of sixteen he went on to set up his own business Empire. He has said that a fresh mind is the cause of much of his success. Just like a child he can see opportunities where adults often see obstacles. This is exactly the mindset that he had when he quit his studies and first set up his first company as a teenager. He let go of ego or judgement and embraced the inner child. He leapt into the unknown. Throughout his career he has maintained that childlike attitude from launching Virgin Records to Virgin Atlantic airline and more. He has even said that there were many times he didn't know what he was doing but just like a child he pushed through and achieved what seemed impossible.

"If your ego and your accomplishments stop you from listening, then they've taught you nothing." Jimmy Iovine.

NEVER GIVE UP

Whatever your goals are you need to persist at them and stay focused. Nothing can take the place of persistence. You might be talented but without persistence you won't get anywhere. Most goals don't come true because people give up. They meet a challenge or setback and they don't persist. There are reasons for that. First and foremost you need to have a reason behind your persistence. No one wants to keep going if they don't care about the result. We need to make sure our goals have meaning and matter to us. Never set goals just to please others or to look good. Really put thought into the why of your goals. Question them and write down why they matter to you. If the why behind them is not strong enough reason then revisit your goals.

Self belief is another reason that people do not achieve their goals. In order to achieve anything we need self belief. Now part of the SMART acronym that we looked at earlier states that goals should be achievable and realistic. But that doesn't mean you should set small goals. They should be something big enough to inspire you and also believable for you to achieve. If it's something too lofty then you're going to get discouraged and you won't persist. To really win, break down a big goal into lots of small goals. Those can be like your milestones on the journey towards the big goal. Staying with the SMART acronym for a moment remember to measure your goals. When we lose sight of how far we've come it can be easy to get discouraged. Through measuring our goal accomplishments it's going to inspire us to motivate us to move forward. Not only will you cultivate persistence you will also cultivate momentum. Get those wins under your belt.

To really ensure your maximum persistence surround yourself with a team of people that will inspire you to move forward. Great achievements have never been achieved alone. there's no such thing as a self-made man or woman. Just think of people like Arnold Schwarzenegger. He was helped by Joe Wilder at the start of his bodybuilding career. Joe introduced him to America, the gyms, trainers, methods and helped to make him a household name. Or think of Taylor Swift who was inspired by Shania Twain's songs. There are two types of relationships that can help you to persist through adversity and achieve your goals.

- *Mentors*

Mentors are a guide to your goals. They are people who have usually gone through the process before and achieved something similar to what you're trying to achieve. They'll be able to look at your strengths and weaknesses from a bird's eye view and pinpoint exactly what you need to do. You might not actually need to have met them in person. They could come from reading biographies, YouTube videos, listening to music and so on.

- *Peers*

Peers are the people at a similar level that are facing similar situations and challenges. They are your friends and colleagues. They will give you confidence and support towards solutions and innovations. With a team of mentors and peers in place it will help you to progress forward even during the most challenging of times.

Vision boards

Vision boards are one of the most valuable tools available to you. They form a visual representation of where you're going. Through feeding your subconscious mind with these images it brings you closer to achieving your destiny. The human mind is easily influenced by visual stimulus and therefore representing your goals using images stimulates your emotions much more than words. After all, words can only say so much. A picture can say much more.

A vision board is a collection of images that represent your goals. The collection can be a cork board with pins of pictures printed out and pinned onto it. Or it could even be something made on your computer and then saved as an image. Regardless of where you store it by placing your goals in visual form it allows you to study them frequently and install them deep into your awareness. This focuses your mind on your goals and attracts you to the right situations and opportunities.

The vision board is the perfect tool for keeping your goals at the top of your mind. Ideally you want to put that vision board somewhere that you can see everyday and that will encourage you to frequently visualise your goals. This is a really important step to take because your subconscious mind is fed by these visions which programme your brain to be aware of opportunities. It will magnetise and attract the right people, opportunities and resources towards achieving your goal. Plus you will become naturally more motivated to reach your goals. Surprisingly you'll find yourself in more situations that bring you closer to your goals. This is all due to programming your subconscious through the visualization.

How to create a vision board

First of all pull up your goals. Start finding pictures that represent those goals, the feelings around them and the experiences. Look through magazines, newspapers and Google to find the right images. Choose images that inspire you and make you feel good. Be selective and tidy about what you put on the board. Don't put too much on there. It should be clear to you. Too many images will dilute your focus. For example if you've always dreamt of having a house by the beach then try to find an image of that that really resonates with you. Or if you've always wanted an amazing body, find a picture of an amazing body and just cut the head off it and put it on your health board. whatever represents that goal to you and whatever speaks and resonates put it in there. Additionally I like to put some affirmations, inspirational words, quotes and so on on the boards. Those can represent how you want to feel. It could be emotions you want to feel on a daily basis such as, happy, loved, healthy, free and so on.

If you're creating a hard copy vision board then print or cut them out. If you are just creating an online canvas then canva is a great tool which is free to use. They have some cool templates to fit your pictures into multiple grids on one page. Personally I have a page for each of my goals with various images of relevance. For example one for the career, one for health and so on. Work on your vision board and regularly update it. Keep those goals you achieved in there also because that proves you can do it.

Everyday take a few moments to contemplate your vision board. Make sure you're getting the full benefit of it so place it somewhere that you'll see every day. I suggest that you take a few minutes to look at it at least twice a day. When you wake up it is a good time and when you go to bed is also a good time. This will make sure that your goals are at the top of your mind when you start the day and that they are programmed into your subconscious while sleeping. If it's a hard copy try leaving it in your bedroom. if it's a data version then you can have it as your desktop background or on your spreadsheet with all your goals inside. Wherever it is just make sure that you see it everyday.

Go ahead and give the vision board a try, you've got nothing to lose. At the very least it will give you an idea of what you're looking for more clearly. That will stop your goals from being so vague. What we focus on expanding our lives. Visualisation is one of the most effective ways to expand on the things that we want to focus on. Get clear on your goals and motivate yourself to bring them into reality.

Write your goals everyday

Writing out your goals every morning is a great way to further install them into your subconscious. There is something about the act of writing goals out by hand that connects the mind and your focus. Numerous studies have proven this. For a number of years I have been doing this. In fact the first thing I do every morning is to write out my top goals. At that time of the day your subconscious mind is primed for manifesting goals.

If you're still not sure of what your goals are you can use this exercise to just write out whatever you want everyday for the next thirty days. At the end of thirty days you will notice that there are some consistently written goals. Those are your main goals.

Affirmations

In the same regard affirmations are another great way to install your goals into your goal seeking subconscious. If you followed the goal setting process in this book so far then your goals should be written in the present tense and in a positive tone. In addition, create more affirmations of the kind of person who would achieve those goals. For example,

Goal = Lose 5 kg. Affirmations = I am 80kg, I am slim and fit, I am healthy
Goal = Double my salary. Affirmations = I am earning 10k usd per month, I am wealthy, I am smart
Goal = Find my perfect partner. Affirmations = I am in a happy relationship, I am the prefer partner, I am confident
Goal = Travel to Egypt. Affirmations = I am travelling to Egypt, I am adveteturus.

You can recite those goals out loud everyday. I suggest doing it every morning and night before bed. You can really go all in it by doing them every hour. Sometimes I do this for ten days. I will have an alarm go off every hour and that will be my cue to recite affirmations or write out my goals. After ten days my mind is much more positively in tune. I invite you to take this challenge.

TEAMS & ACADEMIA & MORE

Goal setting is an important part of any successful organisation. The goals of each employee should align with the goals of the company. Team leaders and managers must take responsibility for communicating the goals of the organization to their team. They also need to encourage employees to set and link their individual goals to align with the vision of the company as a whole.

Setting the right goals for your team is probably the most important part of the goal setting process. Achieving the desired outcome for the company depends on it. Many employees struggle to understand their team's strategies. As a result of this disconnect many don't care. According to research by Robert Kaplan and David Norton less than ten percent of employees fully understand what is expected of them and what their company strategy is. Teams need to drive clear communication of values, goals and vision are integral to a successful culture.

Setting goals for your team is an undeniably important activity to create a united effort towards success. When your team has specific and challenging goals it will inspire higher levels of performance. Everyone will be closer aligned and working towards the same vision. Failure to effectively set goals for your team will result in poor results and productivity of your employees. Your team needs to know why they are given a task where it fits into a larger vision.

Clearly there are some significant benefits to goal setting. Not only will it boost your employee engagement it will also save you time and improve efficiency. Goal setting in your team will make sure the team is all on the same path. They all know what's expected of them and it creates a harmonious culture. Everyone has an equal responsibility and duty. People will have a wide understanding behind the purpose of what they are doing. As such they will take care in what they are doing because they appreciate the value of their work. This will keep your team motivated and encourage them to work harder. Plus the high achievers will be more likely to help out their peers with any issues that may arise.

To further strengthen relationships team leaders should regularly arrange team building activities. Those will break tensions and make the team more comfortable with each other. It will also help the team to understand each other's strengths and weaknesses. At all times open communication must be encouraged and misunderstandings dealt with promptly. The end result for the team is to become better and stronger.

Successfully setting goals in a team depends on having alignment between the objectives of the team and at an individual level. In a nutshell everyone needs to be working towards the same vision. Make sure your team understands the team's goals and encourage them to set goals for themselves and the group. Ask them to consider what they want to achieve and how will it benefit the team? Ensure that they are motivated. Goals shouldn't just be about the outcome it should involve a fulfilling process for all involved. The key is to cover three things, the end result, the measurement and the why.

There are a number of methods you can use when setting goals in teams. The SMART methodology explained earlier is just as effective for setting goals individually as it is for teams. OKR is another method you can use. More on that later. To help you set goals for your team consider using a customised system that has attributes to suit your company.

OKR

OKR (Objectives and Key Results) is a useful and easy to use goal system used by Google and more. The concept originated in Silicon Valley with Google adopting it in 1999. Since then Google has grown from forty employees to over sixty thousand. In addition to Google using OKR, other companies including Walmart, Spotify, Target, Twitter, LinkedIn and more use it.

Through setting measurable goals it can be used to create alignment and engagement. Application of OKR ensures that goals are frequently set, tracked and evaluated. This is perfect in corporate and working environments because it really engages the whole team. Making sure that everyone is headed in the same direction with clarity is a strong advantage of the method.

The formula for OKR requires that a goal describes both what you will achieve and how you will measure it. The goal is the target and how you measure it makes it. Without these components it is just a dream. The formula for OKR goes as follows.

I will _____ as measured by _____.

Fill in the blanks and you have your goal/target and measurement. You can have multiple measures if you need to. For example your goal could be to increase commissions in your company by a certain amount and that could be measured by customer acquisition. Or another example could be a sales target from your advertising campaigns. That could be measured by conversions of the advertising. You could even start to use OKR in your personal life. For example, say you want to have a relationship but your single. That's your goal and measuring it could be from dates you went on. Or one more example could be health. Say you want to gain 5kg of muscle. Well you could measure that goal by weight gain or gym attendance.

As we can see the acronym OKR has two key components. Objectives which are your goals and key results which are your measurements. The objectives should be clear, quality and engaging so that they motivate you and your team. The key results should also be clear, quantitative and measurable. Essentially it should be a number. They can be multiple but not too many otherwise people will get lost in the system.

The uniqueness of OKR is that it can be adapted and tweaked. Instead of the standard static plans that many companies use OKR takes a more flexible approach to goal setting. Through using shorter goal cycles it makes companies much more able to adapt and respond to changes. Not only that but OKR is simple and straightforward to implement. Goals don't need to be a laborious process which is usually the case when more people are involved. OKR reduces the time spent setting goals and as a result their resources are driven towards achievement instead of planning.

Introducing OKR to your team is more of a journey than an event. Changes in culture of a company does not happen overnight. Company dynamics should be modified over a few months as you customize the new system into place. An important part of OKR is to ensure everyone understands what's expected of them at work. The information should be clear to all involved so that everyone moves towards the same goals and is on the same page. When correctly set up, OKRs are a simple process and won't take up much time to implement. In most cases it will only take a few hours each quarter to check and review your OKRs.

OKR Tips

- Typically set during the quarterly planning process.
- Lightweight and not time consuming
- Productivity, focus, and great for company culture.
- Flexible

Objectives:
- Consist of 3-5 high level Objectives.
- Should be simple, short and easy to memorize
- Make sure they are fun and motivate your team.

Key Results:
- Consist of 3-5 measurable Key Results
- Measured by a number or a score, 0-100% or 0 to 1.0.
- Quantifiable, achievable and not impossible.

THE FEEDBACK LOOP

In 1953 it was starting to look impossible that the world's highest mountain, Mount Everest could be climbed. Since 1921 ten attempts to climb the mountain had all failed. Analysis of those failures revealed that the climbers were not taking the right pathway up the mountain. In 1950 a new southern pathway to summit the mountain through Nepal was discovered. A new way had been found through feedback.

The first to attempt through the new pathway was by a Swiss team in 1952. They climbed all the way up to 228,210 feet before going back down. This was the highest anyone had been so far. Their failure to summit the mountain was down to persistence and fitness. Enter a beekeeper Edmund Hillary (later Sir Edmund). At thirty three years old Edmund was a strong candidate. In the past two years he had been on four Himalayan expeditions and was at the prime of his physical fitness. Aware of the shortcomings of the previous exhibitions he came fit, healthy and determined. He also decided to lead his team through a different starting route. Willpower and persistence pushed him through the harsh Khumbu Icefall terrain and onto a new pathway.

Edmund was part of a team who after twelve days reached South Col which is a significant staging area for a final summit push. The day was May 21 which gave them a short period of time before heavy snowfall would obstruct a summit. From the team a former president of the Oxford Mountaineering Club - Tom Bourdillon, and a brain surgeon - Charles Evans, were chosen to attempt the first summit. However at 28,700 feet they ran into oxygen problems. Exhausted both men understood that soon they would run out of oxygen and agreed to go back.

Three days passed, Edmund and local sherpa Tenzing Norgay started their attempt to reach the mountain top. Tenzing was a local Sherpa who was chosen because he had already proven his summit potential. In fact, he was the most experienced and had been at least four thousand feet higher than any of the others had. No one had gone with someone with such experience before. Tenzing had been part of six previous attempts to summit the mountain. He had the feedback and it paid off. Hillary and Tenzing reached the highest point on Earth at 11:30 a.m. on May 29.

So feedback is important. If you want to climb to the top of the mountain and reach your goals then you need some sort of feedback system in place. First of all you need your goals written down. As mentioned earlier that could be in a notepad or it could be in a document on your computer. A computer is much better because you can easily edit it and organize as you progress. But whichever you prefer.
So what does feedback on your goals involve? Fundamentally it's about checking you're on the right path and making progress. Therefore you need to be honest with yourself and question your progress. Make sure you ask the right questions to really probe into how you're doing. Ask yourself what you are doing good, what you are doing bad and what needs to change. In addition, come up with more questions relevant to each of those goals. Let's take a look at some examples.

Health

Let's say your goal is to lose 5kg and get a six pack. Your plan would probably involve some diet to be in a caloric deficit so that you're losing weight. Plus you will have some kind of exercise regime in place. Right there's a few things that you can measure. Then you could start asking yourself some of the following questions. Did I complete my exercise plan for this week? What would I rate myself out of ten this week for my exercise plan? Then you could ask yourself about your diet. Did I stick to my diet? What would I give myself out of ten this week for my diet? Those are just some example questions. You can come up with your own as you wish. Just make sure they give you some useful answers.

Going further you could ask yourself what was good about your progress? What was bad about it? What do you need to do to improve? What changes do you need to make? What habits do you need to implement? What things do you need to stop? What is standing in the way of you achieving your goals? How can you overcome it? Write your answers in a short paragraph and that can be like a summary of how you are progressing. Each month you can keep an eye on your progress and make adjustments as necessary.

Relationships

Okay so let's say that you're single and your goal is to find your ideal partner to be in a relationship with. Some of the things in your goal plan might be to go on dates, build confidence, create an online dating profile and go to two social events a week. Okay, so there are some things which you can measure. Ask yourself, did you go on any dates this week? How did they go? What went well, what went bad and what can you improve? How about your dating profile, is it attracting the right people? What's good about it, what's bad about it and what do you need to change? How about your confidence levels? What would you give them out of ten? How can you raise them? Did you go to any social activities this week? What social activities could you go to next week? Again now you'll have a good summary and understanding of where you are towards achieving your goal. You will know what you need to do to achieve it.

Finance

As an example let's assume that you want to double your income in six months. Part of your plan to double your income could be to find a new side come. You could ask for a pay rise at your job. Also you could find an investment that increases your wealth. So there you have three things that you can measure your progress by. Ask yourself some questions. What actions have you taken towards increasing your income? What questions could you ask that investigate whether you have fulfilled the objective? Have your actions been fruitful? What changes do you need to make? Have you found any side hustles? Did you ask your boss for a pay rise? Have you come up with a good set of reasons to present to your boss as to why he should raise your salary? Have you taken action on making any investments? Why not? What do you need to learn? What you need to do? The quality of your questions will determine the quality of the answers. Come up with a question that will give you a clear picture of what you need to do going forward.

How often should I review my goals?

At the start when it comes to feedback I suggest for you to review your goals every week. Do that for the first six months and then when you get a better understanding of how to review goals you can do it every couple weeks or every month. But always make sure you review them at least once a month.

Okay great, so as you can see the review can give you some key insights into how you are doing and what you need to do going forward. Without this you won't have the right feedback to be able to climb those mountains and succeed in your goals. Be sure to do that regularly and it's even better if you can get help from your peers or mentor to guide you through that process. When you have set some goals it is vital that you frequently review and assess them. This allows you the time to ensure that you're progressing in the right direction and staying relevant.

Reward yourself often

Reward yourself for your successes, but don't punish yourself for failure. before you set a goal identify why you're setting a goal. Reward yourself every single step of the way. When you achieve little tasks, set up a reward. Maybe that's a little holiday somewhere or a day off for some time to enjoy a nice movie. Just make sure that the process to what your goals is a pleasure. Celebrate your wins, even the small ones. This will keep you emotionally engaged in momentum.

CONCLUSION

Congratulations on completing your journey to the end of this book. Goal accomplished! I'm excited that you now have some goals that you're excited about. You've taken a powerful step with goal setting and you're on a path towards a better future. Without those goals you would just be drifting through life. Now you have purpose.

Since we're at the end of this book I want to take a moment to summarise some of the most important topics that were covered. Allow me to refresh those in your mind. First of all we talked about what goal setting is. Goals are something that guide and focus us towards changing our life for the better. This encourages us to achieve a high level of success and become a more self actualised person.

Moving on we talked about how to actually set your goals and what your goals should be. The goal setting process outlined here has four steps. You can find an action guide for that process in the bonus chapter. In brief it is as follows. Step one is to set yourself some goals in different sections of your life and those are.

- Health. Relationships. Friends. Family. Finance. Career. Travel, Passions & Adventure. Lifestyle. Learning. Spirituality/ Mental Health. Giving

In step two you analysed your goals and set time frames for each. Those time frames were.

- 1-month. 3-months. 6-months. 1 year. 5 years. 10 years or more.

At this point you should have quite a few goals and you need to move on to step three. Organising your goals into a spreadsheet or a notebook. At this point you can start to prioritise your goals. As discussed there are some essential parts of goal setting and those are.

- Planning: You're much more likely to stick to your goals when you have a specific plan for them.
- Clarity: Having a clear vision.
- Quantification: Making it measurable.
- Enumeration: Defining tasks.
- SMART+: Make your goals fit into the SMART+ framework. That is they should be specific (S), measurable (M), achievable (A), realistic (R), timebound (T) and positive (+). The human mind is particularly sensitive to negativity and positivity. It's been proven that it's best to put your goals into the positive, present tense.
- Motivation: The gasoline, it is what will encourage you to achieve a goal.
- Time Management: Goal setting relies heavily on being able to manage your time well.
- Flexibility: Not all your plans will go as you expect. A flexible attitude is necessary
- Persistence and focus - Obstacles will also come your way. At those times you're going to need to be persistent, focused and keep moving forward.
- Challenging: Set goals that are a little bit out of your reach. This will keep you engaged.
- Self-regulation: The ability to regulate and manage your emotions.
- Vision: Paint a clear picture in your mind's eye that inspires you.

- Feedback: Track and measure your results. Do it frequently.

With our goals set we then started to look at the obstacles to achievement. Those are caused primarily by the other goals you have which compete against each other. The Four Burners Theory was introduced as a method of considering ways in which we can become more effective towards goal achievement. That means that sometimes we will have to shift the focus of our attention on to other goals and let the other goals simmer in the background. Sometimes you can put other goals in maintenance mode. Maybe for a period of time you choose to focus on one goal and let the other ones stay in maintenance. We also talked about some of the ways that you can outsource various activities to ensure that you are spending your most valuable time on the highest leverage things. All of this requires a ruthless attitude.

At this point in the book you would have some worthwhile goals to focus on. But without a plan in place you will never go anywhere. Here, the when, where and how of accomplishing goals was discussed. Productivity and habits can increase your chances of achieving your goals via a much more streamlined process. Additionally, that includes aligning your environment with your goals. The simple act of keeping a clean and tidy environment with minimal distractions is a surefire way to accomplish your goals.

Following on some further tips for setting your goals were presented. Most goals are possible to achieve but the thing that holds many people back is motivation. In the chapter on motivation we dived deep into how it affects goals. Much is the same with motivation; you will also require persistence to stay on track towards your goals. You might be talented but without persistence you will never get anywhere. In addition, surround yourself with the right people to keep you going. Those can be your mentors and peers. Furthermore you can create vision boards to form visual representations of where you're going. This all feeds your subconscious mind to bring you closer to achieving your destiny. We explored that your human mind is strongly sensitive to visual stimulation and subconscious messages that can be presented through vision boards affirmations and riding out your goals everyday. In summary there are a number of ways that you can stay motivated and those are.

- Set boundaries: Set yourself some simple boundaries that will keep you motivated because you know that there will be a break coming up.
- Break it down: Big goals need to be taken one step at a time. Stay motivated with small wins.
- Minimize distractions: Distractions will keep you from your goals. The truth is focus is not really about optimization it's more about subtraction. Remove or block any distractions.
- Education: If you feel you're not progressing fast enough just ask yourself, do I have the appropriate knowledge? Study the relevant books, enroll yourself in a course or even hire a mentor and acquire all the relevant knowledge .
- Waste no time: Start right now on your goals. Take a definitive action right away. Become motivated by your actions.
- Embrace failure: The successful realize that failure is part of the equation and it doesn't affect their

motivation. It just makes them more motivated to try again and succeed at all costs. Never give up.

Great stuff there to keep you motivated! Moving on the importance of time management was introduced and shown to be an essential skill for goal setting. When you learn how to manage your time you have a much better chance of success. Become great at planning and prioritizing the time you have. Implement a system or try selecting your most important tasks for the next day. Place your activities into four different sections based on urgency and importance. Learn to say no to the things that will take away your time. In addition, cultivate a flexible attitude. Sometimes things will require a different approach. Your plans should not be so rigid that they can't move around natural obstacles and challenges. Plus you need to be open to new opportunities as they come up.

In the last chapter some of the ways that goals can be set in teams, academia and group settings were introduced. In order for team leaders and managers to be successful they need to be able to communicate the goals of their organisation to their team members. Team goals need to be in line with the individual goals of the team to create a harmoniously successful environment. This is undeniably important towards the united effort of success. Specifically the method introduced was the OKR (objectives keys and results) which is a system used by Google and various other leading companies. Through setting measurable goals it can be used to create alignment and engagement in a team. Application of OKR ensures that goals are frequently set, tracked and evaluated. This is perfect in corporate and team working environments because it really engages everyone involved.

Thus making sure that everyone is headed in the same direction with clarity is a strong advantage of the method.

Finally we talked about feedback and how important it is to achieving your goals. without a feedback system in place you'll never know where you are on the pathway to your goals. Feedback can be in a notepad or on a computer. Most of all you need to be consistent with it and make sure that you're tracking your progress. Ensure that you're asking the right questions of yourself and what changes you need to make going forwards. When you reach milestone accomplishments be sure to reward yourself.

Excellent so that is a summary of this book. The truth is that achieving your goals is a journey. It's not only about the destination. Because you don't want to arrive at your goals and then be disappointed. The journey there should be enjoyable. Make sure you consider that when you set your goals.

At the start of this book I promised you that you are capable of achieving goals that go far beyond what you believe is possible. Goal setting is something that can raise the bar of your potential and push you to achieve those things that you didn't think were possible before. If you start small and get some small wins under your belt then you can raise the bar higher and higher. Before you know it you will be far away from where you imagined you could be. Make goals a part of your life and that will come true for you.

Go ahead, give it a try.

Thanks for Reading

What did you think of, ***"Goal Setting Success: The Blueprint To Setting Goals & Achieving Them"?***

I know you could have picked any number of books to read, but you picked this book and for that I am extremely grateful. I hope that it added at value and quality to your everyday life. If so, it would be really nice if you could share this book with your friends and family.

If you enjoyed this book and found some benefit in reading this, I'd like to hear from you and hope that you could take some time to post a review. Your feedback and support will help this author to greatly improve his writing craft for future projects and make this book even better.

I want you, the reader, to know that your review is very important and so, if you'd like to leave a review, all you have to do is click here and away you go. I wish you all the best in your future success!

Thank you and good luck

Oscar Monfort

Other Books By Oscar Monfort

[Quit Your Job: How to Live Out Your Dreams, Pursue The Work You Love & Achieve Financial Freedom](#)

Quitting isn't easy, But if you are thinking about leaving your job then keep reading before you turn in your resignation.

In a 2018 poll, over 50 percent of Americans were found to be "actively disengaged" and having a poor or miserable work experience. If you also are not happy or satisfied at work, then it's time to identify what it is that's making you so unhappy and make changes.

Whether your dream is to start a business, travel, or have more free time for yourself. It doesn't matter if you don't even have a plan yet because this book shows you how.

Take the leap into a better life, discover what you love and make your dreams come true with this book.

https://www.amazon.com/Quit-Your-Job-Achieve-Financial-ebook/dp/B082V12644

[Morning Routine: Skyrocket Your Productivity, Enhance Your Energy & Achieve Your Goals With A Fully Optimized Morning Ritual](#)

Wake Up To Your Full Potential…Even If Your Not A Morning Person!

Are you sick of waking up and not feeling any drive or energy for the day?
Do you snooze until the last possible moment?
Are you always rushing to make it on time to work?

Does any of this seem familiar?
If it does, then it's time for change.

Creating a morning routine for yourself is essential to a successful life. It will give you time to focus on your goals and conquer the day with more energy, mindfulness and strength.

Mark Zuckerberg, Oprah Winfrey, Arianna Huffington and Barack Obama, are just a few examples of famous and successful people with morning routines.
Focused, productive and successful mornings generate focused, productive and successful days — which inevitably create a successful life.

Imagine what it would be like if you no longer need to snooze, rush or feel 'asleep' in the morning. So if your ready to say goodbye to mediocre days and wake up fully energized then read this book.

https://www.amazon.com/Morning-Routine-Skyrocket-Productivity-Optimized-ebook/dp/B07X5L7TLP

BONUS GOAL SETTING GUIDES

The Four Step Goal Setting Process

Step 1:

Divide your life into:

Health. Relationships. Friends. Family. Finance. Career. Travel, Passions & Adventure. Lifestyle. Learning. Spirituality/ Mental Health. Giving.

Brainstorm what you want in each area. No censorship, write as fast as you can. Come up with questions or use some of these prompts.

Do you want to? Feel? How? Try? What? Time? Would you like? How much? How many? Achieve?

Step 2:

Analyse your goals and set time frames for each.

1-month. 3-months. 6-months. 1 year. 5 years. 10 years or more.

Step 3:

- Enter your goals into a spreadsheet or a notebook.
- Prioritise your goals. Eliminate any that are not so important.
- Focus only on the goals that are most important to you.

Step 4:

Get SMART +

Use the S.M.A.R.T. protocol to make sure your goals are optimised.

Specific (S). Measurable (M). Achievable (A). Realistic (R). Timebound (T) and positive (+).

Make a plan

Select your goals and break them down into clearly defined steps.

- Work backwards, step by step from achieving your goal
- Brainstorm and list every action that needs to happen
- Figure out the people, resources and materials that you need
- Identify the daily, weekly or monthly habits that will move you closer
- Study the relevant books, enroll yourself in a course or even hire a mentor and acquire all the relevant knowledge .
- Set time frames and use a calendar to help you.
- Surround yourself with a team of people that will inspire you to move forward. They could come from reading biographies, YouTube videos, listening to music or in person.
- Create a vision board. Start finding pictures that represent those goals, the feelings around them and the experiences.
- Write out your goals everyday.

- Affirmations are another great way to install your goals into your goal seeking subconscious.
- <u>Start right now on your goals.</u>

Keep your plans together in some kind of planner. I recommend Google sheets and a calendar.

Rituals Of The Rich & Famous

Success Tips, Strategies and Habits of The Rich & Famous

Get 4 new strategies every week on how to be more productive, confident, and happy.

Get Access Now